THE ULTIMATE SPICE AND HERB COOKBOOK GUIDE

100 INCREDIBLE RECIPES THAT WILL UNIQUELY ENRICH YOUR DISHES

EDWARD WILKINSON

All rights reserved.

Disclaimer

The information contained in this eBook is meant to serve as a comprehensive collection of strategies that the author of this eBook has done research about. Summaries, strategies, tips and tricks are only recommendation by the author, and reading this eBook will not guarantee that one's results will exactly mirror the author's results. The author of the eBook has made all reasonable effort to provide current and accurate information for the readers of the eBook. The author and its associates will not be held liable for any unintentional error or omissions that may be found. The material in the eBook may include information by third parties. Third party materials comprise of opinions expressed by their owners. As such, the author of the eBook does not assume responsibility or liability for any third party material or opinions. Whether because of the progression of the internet, or the unforeseen changes in company policy and editorial submission guidelines, what is stated as fact at the time of this writing may become outdated or inapplicable later.

The eBook is copyright © 2022 with all rights reserved. It is illegal to redistribute, copy, or create derivative work from this eBook whole or in part. No parts of this report may be reproduced or retransmitted in any reproduced or retransmitted in any forms whatsoever without the writing expressed and signed permission from the author.

TABLE OF CONTENTS

TABLE OF CONTENTS 4
INTRODUCTION 8
HERBED BREAKFAST 10
1. Eggs stuffed with nasturtiums 11
2. Frittata with wild herbs 14
3. Eggs in herb sauce 16
4. Pita of greens, herbs and eggs 19
5. Fresh herb sausage 22

HERBED APPETIZERS 24
6. Baby carrots in herb vinegar 25
7. Artichokes with herbs 27
8. Canapés with lemon-herb glaze 30
9. Fresh herb cheese pizza 33
10. Fresh herb and chive biscuits 35
11. Vietnamese spring rolls 38
12. Fried haloumi cheese 41
13. Herb frittelle 44
14. Herbed shrimp in beer 47
15. Dried figs with herbs 50
16. Easy herb focaccia 52

HERBED CHICKEN AND TURKEY 55
17. Crumbled herbal chicken 56
18. Cream of chicken with herbs 59
19. Apricot Dijon glazed turkey 61
20. Chicken and rice on herb sauce 64
21. Chicken in cream and herb 67
22. Chicken madeira on biscuits 70

23. Chicken soup with herbs 73
24. Chicken with wine and herbs..................................... 76

HERBED PASTA 78

25. Herbal ravioli 79
26. Linguine with mixed herb 82
27. Farfalle with herb sauce 85
28. Egg noodles with garlic 88
29. Cappelini with herb spinach 90
30. Gnocchi with mushroom 93

HERBED SEAFOOD 96

31. Herbal shrimp cream 97
32. Malaysian herbal rice 100
33. Angel hair with smoked salmon 103
34. Codfish with herbs 106
35. Cold poached salmon 109
36. Dill herb fillets 112
37. Crispy baked fish and herbs 114
38. Fettuccine with shrimp 116
39. Mussels with garlic 118
40. Fish Caribbean with wine 121
41. Monkfish with garlicky herb 124

HERBED PORK AND LAMB 126

42. Herbed pork cutlets 127
43. Monastery herbal sausage 130
44. Fillet of lamb with herbs 133

HERBED VEGETABLES 136

45. Asparagus with herb dressing........................... 137
46. Herbed corn casserole....................................... 140
47. Herbed corn scallop... 142

48.	Baked herb rice with pecans	144
49.	Vegetable salad	147
50.	Chickpea and herb salad	150
51.	Summer squash soup	153
52.	Fresh herb and parmesan	156
53.	Herbs vegetable confetti	159
54.	Bavarian herb soup	161
55.	Roasted herb barley	163
56.	Cashew roast with herb stuffing	166
57.	Kasha with dried fruit	169

HERBED DESSERTS 172

58.	Lemon herbal ice cream	173
59.	Herbal jelly	176
60.	Herbal lemon cookies	179
61.	Chicken pot pie with herbs	182
62.	Herbed popover mix	185

HERBED BREADS 187

63.	Herb rolls	188
64.	Garden herb bread	191
65.	Lavender herb bread	194
66.	Cheddar wheat herb crescents	197
67.	Corn meal herb bread	200
68.	Country herb crescents	202

HERBED CONDIMENTS 204

69.	Herbal seasoning	205
70.	Ethiopian herb mix (berbere)	207
71.	Herb salad dressing mix	210
72.	Mixed herb vinegar	213
73.	Mixed herb pesto	215
74.	Mustard-herb marinade	217

75.	HERBAL DESSERT SAUCE	219
76.	CITRUS HERB DRESSING	221
77.	COTTAGE-HERB DRESSING	223
78.	HERBES DE PROVENCE MIX	225
79.	HERB AND OIL MARINADE	227
80.	EASY HERB VINEGARS	229
81.	SORREL-CHIVE PESTO	231
82.	CUCUMBER HERB DRESSING	234
83.	HERBED PECAN RUB	236
84.	ZESTY HERB DRESSING	238
85.	GARLIC-LEMON-HERB RUB	240
86.	DOLCE LATTÉ HERB DIP	242
87.	FRENCH HERB BLEND	245
88.	HERB AND SPICE BUTTER	247
89.	HERBAL VEGETABLE DRESSING	249
90.	BACON, TOMATO AND HERB DIP	252
91.	GARLIC HERB SPREAD	254
92.	CHEVRE WITH HERBS SPREAD	257

HERBED DRINKS 259

93.	SPICY HERBAL LIQUEUR	260
94.	FRUITED HERBAL ICED TEA	263
95.	ICE HERBAL COOLER	265
96.	RASPBERRY HERBAL TEA	270
97.	CARDAMOM TEA	272
98.	SASSAFRAS TEA	274
99.	MORINGA TEA	276
100.	SAGE TEA	279

CONCLUSION 281

INTRODUCTION

Herbs are aromatic edible plants used to add flavour to dishes. Most herbs are used for both culinary and medicinal uses and come from plants that may be used for their leaves, as herbs, and also for their seeds, as spices.

Chefs and home cooks alike use fresh and dried herbs to make both sweet and savory dishes, ranging from rich sauces to light salads and herb-laced baked goods. In addition to their culinary uses, medicinal herbs and their valuable essential oils have been relied on for their health benefits since the middle Ages, ranging from anti-inflammatory and antiviral benefits to skin-clearing topical powers.

When herbs are in season, rejoice in recipes that incorporate heavenly rosemary, basil, dill, mint, oregano, and thyme. Cooking with herbs not only releases great fresh flavors, but also is healthy!

Here, herbs are a main Ingredient, rather than a garnish. Half a cup or more of basil, cilantro, mint, or any other fresh herb can be just the ticket for adding a lively flavor to all sorts of dishes. From chickpea salad with dill to fluffy falafel packed with cilantro and parsley to the most refreshing mint ice cream.

Difference between Using Fresh and Dried Herbs

Fresh herbs are generally preferred over dried herbs for culinary purposes, although there are advantages to using dried herbs. While fresh herbs have a much shorter lifespan, dried herbs can maintain their flavor for up to six months when stored in an airtight container in a dark place at room temperature.

While dried herbs are typically used throughout the cooking process, as prolonged heat and exposure to moisture can draw the flavors out of the herbs, fresh herbs are more commonly added towards the end of the cooking process or as a garnish at the end of cooking.

HERBED BREAKFAST

1. Eggs stuffed with nasturtiums

Yield: 2 serving

Ingredient

- 2 large Hard-boiled eggs
- 4 smalls Nasturtium leaves and tender stems; chopped
- 2 Nasturtium flowers; cut in narrow strips
- 1 Sprig Fresh chervil; chopped
- 1 Sprig Fresh Italian parsley; leaves chopped fine
- 1 Green onion; white and pale-green part
- Extra virgin olive oil
- Fine sea salt; to taste
- Black pepper; coarse ground, to taste
- Nasturtium leaves and Nasturtium flowers

Directions:

Hard-cook eggs in boiling water just until yolks are firm, no longer.

Cut each egg in half lengthwise and carefully remove yolk.

Place yolks an in small bowl and add nasturtium leaves, stems and flowers and chopped chervil, parsley and green onion. Mash with fork, adding enough olive oil to make a paste. Season to taste with sea salt and pepper

Lightly salt egg whites

Gently fill cavities with yolk-herb mixture. Grind some pepper on top. Arrange nasturtium leaves on a plate and place stuffed eggs on top.

Garnish with nasturtium flowers.

2. Frittata with wild herbs

Yield: 1 serving

Ingredient

- ½ kilograms Barba di frate and a bunch of wild mint
- 8 Eggs
- 4 Cloves garlic
- 50 millilitres Extra virgin olive oil
- 100 grams Parmesan cheese; grated
- Salt and freshly ground black pepper

Directions:

Put the oil in a small frying pan with the garlic and bring to the boil.

Remove and discard the garlic, when golden brown. Sauté the Barba di frate in the oil for two minutes, add the eggs which have been lightly beaten with the Parmesan, salt and mint. Stir until it is starting to set. Put into a hot oven until cooked. Turn out on to a platter and serve immediately.

3. Eggs in herb sauce

Yield: 6 serving

Ingredient

- 24 Fresh asparagus spears
- ¼ cup Mayonnaise
- 8 ounces Carton commercial sour cream
- 1 Lemon's juice
- ½ teaspoon Salt and ¼ teaspoon White pepper
- ¼ teaspoon Sugar
- 2 teaspoons Fresh parsley; minced
- 1 teaspoon Fresh dill weed; minced
- 1 teaspoon Fresh chives; minced
- 8 Eggs; hard-cooked, divided
- 12 ounces Package cooked 6" x 4" ham slices

Directions:

Cook asparagus, covered, in boiling water 6 to 8 minutes; drain. Cover and chill.

Combine mayonnaise, sour cream, lemon juice, salt, white pepper, sugar, parsley, minced dill-weed, and chives; mix well. Mash 1 hard-cooked egg; add to mayonnaise mixture, and mix well. Cover and chill.

Place 4 asparagus spears on 2 ham slices. Roll ham around asparagus spears, secure with a wooden pick. Place ham-wrapped asparagus on a serving platter. Slice 6 eggs, arrange slices over ham. Spoon about ¼ cup herb sauce over each serving

Sieve remaining egg. Sprinkle over each serving. Garnish with fresh dill-weed.

4. Pita of greens, herbs and eggs

Yield: 12 serving

Ingredient

- 2 pounds Fresh greens
- Salt
- ½ bunch Fresh parsley; chopped
- ½ bunch Fresh dill; chopped
- 1 Handful fresh chervil; chop.
- ¼ cup Butter or margarine
- 1 bunch Scallions; chopped
- ½ teaspoon Ground allspice
- ½ teaspoon cinnamon and ½ teaspoon Nutmeg
- 2 teaspoons Granulated sugar
- Salt and freshly ground pepper
- 5 Eggs; lightly beaten
- 1 cup Crumbled feta cheese
- ½ cup Milk, or more
- ½ cup Butter (optional); melted
- 12 Commercial phyllo sheets

Directions:

Combine the spinach in a large bowl with the parsley, dill, and chervil and mix thoroughly. Heat the ¼ cup butter in a large frying pan, add the scallions to the butter and sauté them until the white parts are translucent.

Add the greens, the spices, sugar, and enough salt and pepper for seasoning.

Now we add the eggs, feta, and enough milk to saturate the greens. Spread 6 phyllo sheets, brushing each with melted butter. Pour in the filling, spreading evenly. Bake for 45 minutes.

5. Fresh herb sausage

Yield: 2 pounds

Ingredient

- 4 Feet small hog casings
- 2 pounds Whitefish fillets, cubed
- 1 Egg, beaten
- 2 tablespoons Chopped fresh chives
- 1 tablespoon Chopped fresh parsley
- 1 teaspoon Lemon juice
- ½ teaspoon Celery salt
- ½ teaspoon Black pepper

Directions:

Prepare casings. Put fish in food processor and pulse just until the fish is broken. Add remaining Ingredients and process just until everything is well blended. Stuff casings and twist off into 3-4" lengths.

HERBED APPETIZERS

6. Baby carrots in herb vinegar

Yield: 1 serving

Ingredient

- 20 smalls Carrots
- ¾ cup Sugar
- 1 tablespoon Lemon juice
- 1 tablespoon Butter
- 2 tablespoons Tarragon vinegar

Directions:

Place carrots, water and lemon juice in small saucepan.

Cover and simmer 5 minutes.

Remove cover, increase heat to high and cook, stirring, until liquid evaporates (5 minutes). Turn heat down.

7. Artichokes with herbs

Yield: 4 serving

Ingredient

- 2 large Artichokes (or 4 medium)
- 1 small Carrot
- 1 small Onion
- 1 tablespoon Olive oil
- 2 tablespoons Parsley; chopped
- ½ teaspoon Basil leaves, dried
- ½ teaspoon Oregano
- ½ teaspoon Dill weed
- 1 Garlic clove
- Salt
- 1 cup Wine, dry white
- Pepper to taste

Directions:

In blender, combine carrot, onion, parsley, dried herbs, garlic and salt and black pepper to taste; process until finely chopped. Stuff herb mixture between leaves of artichokes

Place cooking rack, wine and $\frac{1}{2}$ cup water in 4- or 6-qt pressure cooker. Place artichokes on rack; close cover securely. Place pressure regulator on vent pipe.

Cook 20 minutes at 15 pounds pressure.

8. Canapés with lemon-herb glaze

Yield: 1 serving

Ingredient

- Pumpernickel bread with cream cheese and sliced smoked salmon
- Buttered salty rye with sliced egg and caviar
- Salty rye with horseradish; chili sauce; tiny shrimp
- 1⅔ cup Water
- ⅛ teaspoon Peppercorns
- ½ Bay leaf
- ½ teaspoon Dried dill
- 1 pack (3-oz.) lemon flavoured gelatin
- 1 dash Cayenne pepper
- 3 tablespoons Vinegar

Directions:

Place on a rack and top each canapé with 2 to 3 tablespoons Lemon-Herb Glaze.

Lemon-Herb Glaze: Bring water to simmer; add pepper corns, bay leaf, and dried dill. Cover, and simmer for about 10 minutes. Strain. Dissolve gelatin, salt, and cayenne in the hot liquid. Add vinegar. Chill until slightly thickened. Spoon mixture over canapés

9. Fresh herb cheese pizza

Yield: 8 serving

Ingredient

- 1 tablespoon Cornmeal
- 1 can (10-oz.) All-ready Pizza Crust
- 1 tablespoon Olive oil or oil
- 1 Clove garlic; minced
- 6 ounces Shredded Mozzarella cheese
- ½ cup Grated Parmesan cheese
- 1 tablespoon Chopped fresh basil
- 1 tablespoon Chopped fresh oregano

Directions:

Grease 12-inch pizza pan or 13x9-inch pan; sprinkle with cornmeal. Unroll dough; press into greased pan.

In small bowl, combine oil and garlic; drizzle over dough. Top evenly with mozzarella cheese, Parmesan cheese, basil and oregano.

Bake at 425 for 13-16 minutes or until crust is deep golden brown

10. Fresh herb and chive biscuits

Ingredient

- 8 ounces Firm silken tofu
- ⅓ cup Apple juice
- 1 tablespoon Lemon juice
- 1 cup Whole-wheat flour
- 1 cup All-purpose flour
- 2 teaspoons Baking powder
- ½ teaspoon Baking soda
- ¼ teaspoon Salt, optional
- 2 tablespoons Basil, chopped -=OR=-
- 1 tablespoon Basil, dried
- 2 tablespoons Chives, chopped -=OR=-
- 1 tablespoon Chives, dried

Directions:

Preheat oven to 450F and oil cookie sheets.

Blend tofu till smooth. Blend in apple juice and lemon juice. Transfer to a medium sized mixing bowl and set aside. Sift together the next 5 Ingredients and fold into the tofu mixture. Stir in basil and chives. Turn dough out onto a lightly floured board and form into a ball. Roll dough out to $\frac{1}{2}$" thickness and cut with a cookie cutter. Bake for 12 minutes and serve immediately.

11. Vietnamese spring rolls

Yield: 1 serving

Ingredient

- 1 Red snapper
- 2 tablespoons Fish sauce
- 2 tablespoons Honey
- ½ teaspoon Asian sesame oil
- 40 Rice paper wrappers
- Mint and fresh cilantro
- Thin slices English cucumber
- ½ pounds Fresh bean sprouts
- lettuce leaves
- ¼ cup Rice vinegar
- ¼ cup Lime juice
- ¼ cup Sugar
- ¼ teaspoon Hot Asian chili sauce

Directions:

Combine fish sauce with honey and sesame oil. Rub into fish. Roast at 425F/210C for 40 to 45 minutes.

In a small serving bowl, combine Ingredients for sauce.

Break off a piece of fish and place in the center of each wrapper just below the middle. Add mint and cilantro, 1 slice of cucumber and some bean sprouts on top of fish. Drizzle sauce.

12. Fried haloumi cheese

Yield: 1 serving

Ingredient

- 4 Ripe plum tomatoes
- 1 Red onion
- 1 Cucumber
- 20 Black olives; pitted
- 1 bunch Flat parsley
- 100 grams Haloumi cheese
- Basil; finely chopped
- Coriander; finely chopped
- Chervil
- Chives
- 200 milliliters Olive oil
- 2 Lemons; juice of
- 1 tablespoon White wine vinegar
- Salt and pepper

Directions:

Mix all these together in a bowl with the onions and some flat parsley. Dress with some olive oil and salt and pepper.

In a hot non-stick pan, fry the Haloumi cheese with no oil.

Place on top of the salad and drizzle herb oil around the plate. Now add some lemon juice.

13. Herb frittelle

Yield: 1 serving

Ingredient

- 1 pounds Mixed herb salad leaves
- ¼ cup Freshly grated parmesan
- 3 Free range eggs; lightly beaten
- 1 cup Fresh breadcrumbs
- 2 tablespoons Unsalted butter
- Sunflower oil
- Salt and freshly ground pepper

Directions:

Place herb leaves in a medium bowl. Stir in the onion, basil, parmesan, breadcrumbs, eggs and seasoning.

Melt the butter in a large frying pan. Add enough oil so that there is ¼ inch of oil in the pan. Using 1 generous Tablespoons of the mixture for each fritter, fry the frittelle a few at a time until deeply golden, about 3 minutes each side.

Drain on kitchen paper; keep warm in a low oven until the remaining frittelle are cooked.

14. Herbed shrimp in beer

Yield: 6 servings

Ingredient

- 2 pounds Peeled raw shrimp
- 1½ cup Great western beer
- 2 Cloves Garlic, minced
- 2 tablespoons Chives, snipped
- 2 tablespoons Parsley, snipped
- 1½ teaspoon Salt
- ½ teaspoon Pepper
- Shredded lettuce
- 2 Green onions, finely chopped

Directions:

Combine all Ingredients except lettuce and green onions in a bowl.

Cover, refrigerate 8 hours or overnight; stir occasionally. Drain, reserve marinade

Broil shrimp 4 inches from heat until cooked and tender.

Do not overcook or shrimp will become tough. Brush occasionally with marinade.

Serve shrimp on shredded lettuce; sprinkle with chopped green onion.

15. Dried figs with herbs

Yield: 4 servings

Ingredient

- ½ pounds Dried figs
- ½ pounds Dried cranberries
- 2 cups Red wine
- ¼ cup Lavender or flavored honey
- Spices tied in cheesecloth:

Directions:

Add figs to a saucepan with red wine and honey and cheesecloth with a selection of herbs. Bring to a simmer and cook, covered, for 45 minutes or until really tender.

Remove figs from saucepan; boil the liquid down until about more than half remains.

Discard spices in cheesecloth. Serve as is or, spoon over vanilla sherbet or ice milk.

16. Easy herb focaccia

Yield: 24 serving

Ingredient

- 16 ounces Packaged Hot Roll Mix
- 1 Egg
- 2 tablespoons Olive Oil
- ⅔ cup Red Onion; Finely Chopped
- 1 teaspoon Dried Rosemary; Crushed
- 2 teaspoons Olive Oil

Directions:

Lightly grease two round baking pans.

Prepare hot roll mix according to package directions for basic dough, using the 1 egg and substituting the 2 Tablespoons oil for the margarine called for on the package. Knead dough; allow to rest as directed. If using round baking pans, divide dough in half; roll into two 9-inch rounds. Place in prepared pan.

Cook onion and rosemary in a skillet in the 2 teaspoons of hot oil till tender. With fingertips, press indentations every inch or so in the dough

Bake in a 375-degree oven for 15 to 20 minutes or till golden. Cool 10 minutes on a wire rack. Remove from pan and cool completely.

HERBED CHICKEN AND TURKEY

17. Crumbled herbal chicken

Yield: 2 serving

Ingredient

- 2 cups Bread crumbs
- 1 teaspoon Salt
- 1 teaspoon Freshly ground pepper
- 2 tablespoons Dried parsley
- 1 teaspoon Dried marjoram
- 1 teaspoon Dried thyme
- 1 teaspoon Dried oregano
- 1 teaspoon Garlic powder
- 1 Orange; sliced
- 4 Chicken breast halves boned and skinned
- 2 Eggs; beaten OR Egg substitute
- 2 tablespoons Butter or margarine
- 2 tablespoons Vegetable oil
- 1 cup Chicken stock or white wine
- 1 Sprig fresh parsley

Directions:

Place bread crumbs, salt, pepper, parsley, marjoram, thyme, oregano, and garlic powder in a food processor and grind thoroughly. Dip the chicken breasts into the beaten egg and then coat with bread crumbs.

Over medium-high heat, brown the chicken breasts on both sides in butter and oil. Lower the heat, add stock or wine, and cover. Simmer for 20 to 30 minutes, depending on the thickness of the breasts.

Garnish with orange slices and parsley.

18. Cream of chicken with herbs

Yield: 1 serving

Ingredient

- 1 can Cream of Chicken Soup
- 1 can Chicken Broth
- 1 can Milk
- 1 can Water
- 2 cups Bisquick Baking Mix
- $\frac{3}{4}$ cup Milk

Directions:

Empty cans of soup into large pan

Stir in cans of water and milk. Mix together till smooth. Heat on medium heat until boiling

Stir together Bisquick and milk. Dough should be thick and sticky. Drop dough by teaspoonfuls into boiling soup.

Cook dumplings for approx. 8 to 10 minutes. uncovered

19. Apricot Dijon glazed turkey

Yield: 6 serving

Ingredient

- 6 Chicken bouillon cubes
- 1½ cup Uncooked long-grain white rice
- ½ cup Slivered almonds
- ½ cup Chopped dried apricots
- 4 Green onions with tops; sliced
- ¼ cup Snipped fresh parsley
- 1 tablespoon Orange zest
- 1 teaspoon Dried rosemary; crushed
- 1 teaspoon Dried thyme leaves
- 1 Boneless turkey breast half -about 2 1/2 pounds
- 1 cup Apricot jam or orange marmalade
- 2 tablespoons Dijon mustard

Directions:

For herbed pilaf, bring water to a boil. Add bouillon. Remove from heat to a bowl. Add all remaining pilaf Ingredients except turkey; mix well. Place Turkey on top of rice mixture.

Cover and Bake 45 minutes

Remove turkey from oven; carefully remove Baker with Oven Mitts.

Stir pilaf just before serving, serve with turkey and sauce.

20. Chicken and rice on herb sauce

Yield: 4 serving

Ingredient

- ¾ cup Hot water
- ¼ cup White wine
- 1 teaspoon Chicken flavored bouillon granules
- 4 (4 oz.) chicken breast halves skinned and boned
- ½ teaspoon Cornstarch
- 1 tablespoon Water
- 1 pack Neufchatel-style cheese with herbs and spices
- 2 cups Hot cooked long grain rice

Directions:

Bring hot water, wine and bouillon granules to a boil in large skillet over medium-high heat. Reduce heat and add chicken, simmer 15 minutes; turning after 8 minutes. Remove chicken when done, keep warm. Bring cooking liquid to boil, reduce to ⅔ cup.

Combine cornstarch and water and add to liquid. Bring to boil and cook 1 minute, stirring constantly. Add cream cheese and cook until well blended, stirring constantly with wire whisk. To serve:

Top rice with chicken, spoon sauce over chicken

21. Chicken in cream and herb

Yield: 6 serving

Ingredient

- 6 Chicken thighs, skinned and boned
- All-purpose flour seasoned with salt and pepper
- 3 tablespoons Butter
- 3 tablespoons Olive oil
- ½ cup Dry white wine
- 1 tablespoon Lemon juice
- ½ cup Whipping cream
- ½ teaspoon Dried thyme
- 2 tablespoons Minced fresh parsley
- 1 Lemon, sliced (garnish)
- 1 tablespoon Capers, rinsed and drained (garnish)

Directions:

In a large skillet, heat 1½ tablespoons each butter and oil. Add pieces of chicken as will fit without crowding. Cook

Add wine and lemon juice to skillet and simmer over moderately high heat, stirring to blend in browned particles. Boil, reducing to about half

Add whipping cream, thyme, and parsley; boil until sauce thickens slightly. Pour any meat juices from warming platter into sauce.

Adjust sauce for seasoning to taste. Pour over meat and garnish with parsley, lemon slices and capers

22. Chicken madeira on biscuits

Yield: 6 serving

Ingredient

- 1½ pounds Chicken breast
- 1 tablespoon Cooking oil
- 2 Cloves garlic, minced
- 4½ cup Quartered fresh mushrooms
- ½ cup Chopped onion
- 1 cup sour cream
- 2 tablespoons All-purpose flour
- 1 cup Skim milk
- ½ cup Chicken broth
- 2 tablespoons Madeira or dry sherry

Directions:

Cook chicken in hot oil over medium-high heat for 4 - 5 minutes or till no longer pink. Add garlic, mushrooms and onion to skillet. Cook, uncovered, for 4 - 5 minutes or till liquid evaporates.

In a bowl stir together sour cream, flour, ½ teaspoon salt and ¼ teaspoon pepper. Add sour cream mixture, milk, and broth to skillet. Add chicken and Madeira or sherry; heat through.

Serve over Herbed Biscuits.

Sprinkle with thinly sliced green onions if desired

23. Chicken soup with herbs

Yield: 7 serving

Ingredient

- 1 cup Dried cannellini beans
- 1 teaspoon Olive oil
- 2 Leeks, trimmed -- washed
- 2 Carrots -- peeled and diced
- 10 milliliters Garlic -- finely chopped
- 6 Plum tomatoes -- seeded and
- 6 New potatoes
- 8 cups Home-made Chicken Broth
- ¾ cup Dry white whine
- 1 Sprig fresh thyme
- 1 Sprig fresh rosemary
- 1 Bay leaf

Directions:

Rinse beans and pick over, cover with water and set aside to soak for 8 hours or overnight. In a large pot, heat oil over medium-low heat. Add leeks, carrots and garlic; cook until softened, about 5 minutes. Stir in tomatoes and cook for 5 minutes. Add potatoes and cook for 5 minutes.

Add chicken broth, wine and herbs; bring to a boil. Drain the beans and add to the pot; cook 2 hours, or until the beans are soft.

Remove the bay leaf and herb sprigs before serving.

24. Chicken with wine and herbs

Yield: 4 serving

Ingredient

- Frying chicken
- ½ teaspoon Oregano
- ½ teaspoon Basil
- 1 cup Dry white wine
- ½ teaspoon Garlic salt
- ½ teaspoon Salt
- ¼ teaspoon Pepper

Directions:

Wash chicken and cut up. In small amount of Oil, brown chicken pieces on all sides. Pour off excess Oil. Add Wine and seasoning and simmer for 30 to 40 minutes or until chicken is tender.

HERBED PASTA

25. Herbal ravioli

Ingredient

- 2 8.5x11" fresh pasta sheets
- 1¼ cup Ricotta cheese; fat free
- ¾ cup Italian bread crumbs
- ¼ cup Fresh basil and ¼ cup Fresh parsley; chopped
- ⅛ teaspoon oreganoo and ⅛ Nutmeg
- Salt and Black pepper
- Poached tomato base
- 2 large Tomatoes; ripe
- 2 Cloves garlic; thinly sliced
- 6 Fresh basil leaves

Directions:

In large mixing bowl, combine ricotta, bread crumbs, basil, parsley, oregano, nutmeg, salt and black pepper.

Lay pasta sheets flat on work surface and drop four equal portions (about $\frac{1}{4}$ cup) of ricotta mixture onto the 4 quadrants on the left half only of each sheet of pasta. Fold right half of pasta sheet over other half. Press down around each cheese mound to seal.

Bring water to boil in large pot. Drop ravioli into water and boil 3-5 minutes. Wash, core, peel and rough-chop tomatoes. Set aside. Briefly sauté garlic, Add tomatoes, basil, water and salt

Cover and cook 5 minutes. Spoon tomato mixture onto 4 serving plates and top each plate with two raviolis.

26. Linguine with mixed herb

Yield: 1 serving

Ingredient

- 4 mediums Carrots
- 3 mediums Zucchini
- 1 pounds Dried linguine
- 1 cup Packed fresh flat-leafed parsley leaves
- ½ cup Packed fresh basil leaves
- 1 tablespoon Fresh thyme leaves
- 1 tablespoon Fresh rosemary leaves
- 1 tablespoon Fresh tarragon leaves
- ½ cup Freshly grated Parmesan
- ⅓ cup Olive oil
- ¼ cup Walnuts; toasted golden
- 1 tablespoon Balsamic vinegar

Directions:

In a 6-quart kettle bring 5 quarts salted water to a boil. Add linguine and cook 8 minutes, or until barely tender. Add carrots and cook 1 minute. Add zucchini and cook 1 minute. Reserve ⅔ cup cooking water and drain pasta and vegetables.

In a large bowl stir together pesto and reserved hot cooking water. Add pasta and vegetables and toss well.

In a food processor blend together all **Ingredient**s with salt and pepper to taste until smooth.

27. Farfalle with herb sauce

Yield: 1 serving

Ingredient

- 2 cloves garlic -- minced
- 1 lb. farfalle -- cooked
- 2 c fresh mint sprigs
- ¾ extra virgin olive oil
- ½ c vegetable stock
- 1½ tsp salt
- ½ tsp fresh pepper
- 1 Tablespoons lemon juice
- ½ c walnuts, toasted, chopped
- ½ c Parmesan cheese

Directions:

In a blender, or food processor, add the herbs and garlic, and while the machine is running, drizzle in ½ olive oil, the vegetable stock, and then the rest of the oil. Add salt, pepper and lemon, blend and taste and adjust seasoning.

Toss with cooked pasta while still warm, fold in nuts and cheese. Garnish with fresh herb sprigs.

28. Egg noodles with garlic

Yield: 4 serving

Ingredient

- ½ pounds Egg noodles
- 4 large Garlic clove(s)
- 1½ cup Mixed herbs
- 2 tablespoons Extra-virgin olive oil
- Salt and pepper

Directions:

Cook the pasta in a large pot of boiling, salted water until tender but still firm, 7-9 minutes. Drain well.

Meanwhile, chop the garlic, Mince the herbs; you'll have about 1 cup.

Combine the olive oil and garlic in a large frying pan. Cook over medium heat, stirring occasionally, until the garlic is fragrant but not browned, 2-3 minutes. Remove from the heat and stir in the minced herbs.

Add the cooked noodles to the frying pan and toss. Season with salt and pepper to taste and toss well

29. Cappelini with herb spinach

Yield: 6 serving

Ingredient

- 8 ounces Angel hair pasta(cappelini)
- 10 ounces frozen spinach
- 1 pounds Fresh spinach
- 1 tablespoon Virgin olive
- 1 Onion; chopped
- 2 tablespoons Fresh parsley
- ½ teaspoon Dried leaf basil
- ½ teaspoon Dried leaf oregano
- ½ teaspoon Ground nutmeg
- Salt and pepper to taste
- 2 tablespoons Grated Parmesan cheese;

Directions:

Bring a large kettle of water to a boil and cook pasta until al dente, 3 minutes. Drain in a colander; set aside. Meanwhile place frozen spinach in a steamer rack over boiling water until slightly wilted.

In a non-stick skillet, heat oil and Sauté onion until softened. Place spinach, onion, parsley, basil, oregano, nutmeg, salt and pepper in a blender of a food processor fitted with metal blade, and process to purée. Place pasta in a serving bowl, toss with sauce and sprinkle with Parmesan cheese

30. Gnocchi with mushroom

Yield: 3 servings

Ingredient

- 2 large baking potatoes
- 2 eggs
- 1 cup flour; or less
- 1 salt; to taste
- 1 tablespoon butter
- 1 cup sliced shiitake mushrooms
- 1 cup tomato concasse
- chopped basil/ parsley/chives
- 1 parmesan cheese; for garnish

Directions:

With a fork, prick potatoes all over; bake until tender, 45 minutes to 1 hour. Remove and add eggs, then add enough flour. Season to taste with salt and pepper

Transfer dough to a pastry bag and pipe out long cylinders. Chill until firm. Cut each cylinder into 1-inch pieces. Lightly flour work surface and roll pieces, one at a time, over prongs of a fork, or over a gnocchi dowel. Boil.

Toss with mushroom mixture and herbs;

HERBED SEAFOOD

31. Herbal shrimp cream

Yield: 4 serving

Ingredient

- ½ Stick unsalted butter
- 4 mediums Shallots; finely chopped
- 1-quart Heavy cream
- 2 cups Dry white wine
- 1 pounds Shrimp; bay, small, peeled
- 1 tablespoon Lemon juice
- 1 tablespoon Dill
- 1 tablespoon Tarragon; finely chopped
- 2 teaspoons Parsley
- 2 teaspoons Chives; finely chopped
- ¾ teaspoon Salt

Directions:

In a large saucepan or skillet, melt the butter over moderate heat. Add the shallots and sauté ,until tender, 2-3 minutes.

Add the cream and white wine, raise the heat, and boil briskly until the sauce is thick and reduced by about one half, 15-20 minutes while stirring constantly to prevent burning on bottom.

Stir in shrimp and remaining Ingredients. Simmer until heated through, 1 to 2 minutes.

32. Malaysian herbal rice

Ingredient

- 400 grams Fresh salmon
- 2 tablespoons soy sauce and 2 tablespoons Mirin
- 6 cups Cooked jasmine rice
- Kaffir lime leaves
- ½ cup Toasted; shredded coconut
- Turmeric/galangal; peeled
- 3 tablespoons Fish sauce

Dressing

- 2 smalls Red chilies; seeded and minced
- ½ cup Thai basil
- ½ cup Vietnamese mint
- 1 Ripe avocado; peeled
- 1 Red chilli; minced
- 2 Cloves garlic; minced
- ⅓ cup Lime juice

Directions:

Mix the soy and mirin and pour over the fish and marinate for 30 minutes. Heat a grill pan or griller then cook the fish until golden.

Julienne the turmeric, galangal, chilli and kaffir lime leaves and mix with the cooked rice. Add the toasted coconut, basil and mint and mix with the fish sauce. Set aside.

Purée all the dressing Ingredients, then fold the dressing through the rice until the rice is coloured pale green. Flake the cooked fish and add to the rice.

33. Angel hair with smoked salmon

Yield: 4 serving

Ingredient

- 8 ounces Angel hair pasta; uncooked
- 6 ounces Smoked salmon; thinly sliced
- 3 tablespoons Olive oil
- 1 large Garlic; finely chopped
- 2¼ cup Chopped; seeded tomatoes
- ½ cup Dry white wine
- 3 tablespoons Drained large capers
- 1½ teaspoon Spice Islands Dill Weed
- 1½ teaspoon Spice Islands Sweet Basil
- ½ cup Parmesan cheese; freshly grated
- 2 cups tomatoes, wine

Directions:

Prepare pasta according to package directions.

Meanwhile, cut salmon, along the grain, into ½-inch wide strips; set aside.

In large skillet, heat oil over medium-high heat until hot; cook and stir garlic until golden.

Stir capers, dill and basil; cook until mixture is hot, stirring occasionally.

In large bowl, combine pasta and tomato mixture; toss to combine.

Add salmon and cheese; toss lightly. Garnish with remaining tomatoes and parsley, if desired.

34. Codfish with herbs

Yield: 4 serving

Ingredient

- 3 cups Water
- ½ cup Sliced celery
- 1 pack Instant chicken broth
- ½ Lemon
- 2 tablespoons Dehydrated onion flakes
- 1 teaspoon Fresh parsley, chopped
- ½ each Bay leaf
- ⅛ teaspoon Ground cloves
- ⅛ teaspoon Thyme
- 4 each boned and skinned cod steaks
- 2 mediums Tomatoes, cut in half
- 2 mediums Green peppers, seeded and cut in half

Directions:

In a 12-inch skillet, combine water, celery, broth mix, lemon, onion flakes, parsley, bay leaf, cloves and thyme. Bring to a boil, then reduce heat to a simmer. Add fish and poach 5 to 7 minutes. Add tomato and green pepper halves, and finish cooking until fish flakes easily. Remove fish and vegetables, keep warm.

Cook liquid until reduced by half. Remove lemon and bay leaf. Place liquid and half of the cooked tomato and peppers in a blender container. Purée until smooth

Pour over fish and remaining tomato and peppers.

35. Cold poached salmon

Yield: 1 serving

Ingredient

- 6 Skinless; (6ounce) salmon fillets
- Salt and white pepper
- 3 cups Fish stock or clam juice
- 1 bunch Oregano
- 1 bunch Basil
- 1 bunch Parsley
- 1 bunch Thyme
- 6 Tomatoes; peeled, seeded, and diced
- ½ cup Extra virgin olive oil
- 1½ teaspoon Salt
- ½ teaspoon Freshly ground black pepper

Directions:

Season salmon all over with salt and pepper

Bring stock or juice to a boil in a large oven-proof skillet. Add fish, so they are barely touching, and bring liquid back to a boil. Transfer to oven and bake 5 minutes while turning fish over

To make dressing, remove stems and finely chop all herbs. Mix all Ingredients in a small bowl, and reserve in refrigerator.

36. Dill herb fillets

Yield: 4 serving

Ingredient

- 2 pounds fillet of red snapper
- ¾ teaspoon salt
- ½ teaspoon ground pepper
- ½ cup olive oil
- 1½ tablespoon minced parsley
- 1 tablespoon minced shallots, spice
- 1 x hunter freeze dried or fresh
- 1 pinch oregano
- ¼ cup fresh squeezed lemon juice

Directions:

Arrange fish in a single layer, oiled, shallow baking dish. Sprinkle with oil, parsley, shallots, Dill Weed, and oregano. Bake in a preheated oven at 350 degrees F until flesh barely separates when tested with a fork--15 to 20 minutes. Baste twice with pan juices while baking. Remove fish to a serving dish.

Blend lemon juice into pan drippings, then pour over fish.

37. Crispy baked fish and herbs

Yield: 4 serving

Ingredient

- 4 each Fillets white fish
- 1 tablespoon Water
- $\frac{1}{8}$ teaspoon Lemon pepper
- 1 teaspoon Low fat margarine, melted
- 1 each Egg white
- $\frac{1}{2}$ cup Cornflake crumbs
- 2 teaspoons Chopped fresh parsley

Directions:

Preheat oven 400F. Lightly spray a medium size shallow baking pan with vegetable spray. Rinse fish and pat dry.

In small bowl, beat egg white with a little water. Dip fish in egg white, then roll in crumbs. Arrange fish in baking pan. Sprinkle with lemon pepper and parsley, then drizzle margarine over all.

Bake uncovered 20 min or until fish flakes easily

38. Fettuccine with shrimp

Yield: 2 serving

Ingredient

- 1 pack Lipton creamy herb soup mix
- 8 ounces Shrimp
- 6 ounces Fettuccini, cooked
- $1\frac{3}{4}$ cup Milk
- $\frac{1}{2}$ cup Peas
- $\frac{1}{4}$ cup Parmesan, grated

Directions:

Mix soup mix with milk and bring to boiling. Add shrimp and peas and simmer 3 minutes until shrimp are tender. Toss with hot noodles and cheese. Makes 2 serving.

39. Mussels with garlic

Yield: 1 serving

Ingredient

- 1 kilograms Fresh live mussels
- 2 Shallots or 1 small onion
- 200 milliliters Dry white wine
- 1 Bay leaf
- 1 Sprig parsley
- 125 grams Butter
- 1 tablespoon Chopped parsley; up to 2
- 2 Cloves garlic; crushed
- Freshly ground black pepper
- 2 tablespoons Fresh white breadcrumbs to finish
- 250 grams Sea salt for presentation

Directions:

Chop the onion and place it in a good sized pan with the wine, bay leaf, thyme and parsley then bring them to simmering point. Add the mussels, checking that they are closed and discard any that are open. Cover the pan and simmer for 5 or 6 minutes or until the mussels are open.

Beat the butter and thoroughly blend in the parsley and garlic with a little black pepper. Place 1/2tsp on each mussel, add a light sprinkling of breadcrumbs and place under a hot grill for 2-3 minutes.

Serve the mussels hot on the bed of sea salt.

40. Fish Caribbean with wine

Yield: 1 serving

Ingredient

- 1 cup Rice or couscous -- cooked
- 4 Sheets parchment paper, foil
- 2 smalls Zucchini
- 1 Chile poblano
- Pasillo -- in thin strips
- 1 pounds Boneless firm white fish
- 4 mediums Tomatoes
- 10 Black olives
- 1 teaspoon Each chopped fresh basil
- Thyme -- tarragon
- Parsley, and green onion
- 1 Egg

Directions:

Place on a baking sheet and cook for 12 minutes or until fish is done! Place ½ cup of the cooked rice in the middle.

Top each serving with ½ cup of zucchini strips, a piece of the fish, ¼ cup diced tomato and 3 thin strips of the Chile.

Sprinkle a fourth of the chopped olives on each serving, and top with ¼ each of the fresh herbs.

Combine all the sauce Ingredients and purée. Pour into a small saucepan and bring to boil over medium heat. Strain

41. Monkfish with garlicky herb

Yield: 4 serving

Ingredient

- 700 grams Filleted monkfish tails
- 85 grams Butter
- 2 Cloves garlic -- crushed
- Egg (beaten)
- Juice of one lemon
- 1 teaspoon Finely chopped herbs
- Seasoned flour

Directions:

Soften butter and add herbs and garlic. Chill. -- Make a slit in each Monkfish fillet and pack with the chilled herb butter. Fold up to enclose butter. Toss each piece in seasoned flour, dip in beaten egg and roll in breadcrumbs. Press the crumbs firmly onto the fish.

Place the fish in a buttered dish. Dribble a little melted butter or oil, and lemon juice, on top. Cook for 30-35 minutes at 375F/190C.

Serve at once.

HERBED PORK AND LAMB

42. Herbed pork cutlets

Yield: 4 serving

Ingredient

- 1 Egg
- ⅓ cup Dry bread crumbs
- ¼ cup Fresh basil, chopped
- 2 tablespoons Fresh oregano, chopped
- 1 tablespoon Parmesan, fresh grated
- 1 teaspoon Fresh thyme, chopped
- ½ teaspoon Pepper
- ¼ teaspoon Salt
- 1 pounds Fast-fry pork cutlets
- 2 tablespoons Vegetable oil

Directions:

In shallow dish, lightly beat egg. In separate shallow dish, stir together bread crumbs, basil, oregano, Parmesan, thyme, pepper and salt. Dip pork into egg to coat well; press into bread crumb mixture, turning to coat all over.

In large skillet, heat half of the oil. Over medium heat; cook pork, in batches and adding remaining oil if necessary, turning once, for 8-10 minutes or until just a hint of pink remains inside. Serve with new red potatoes and yellow beans.

43. Monastery herbal sausage

Yield: 1 serving

Ingredient

- 400 grams Lean pork
- 400 grams Lean beef
- 200 grams Green pork back fat or fatty
- Pork belly without skin
- 20 grams Salt
- 2 teaspoons finely ground White pepper
- 1 teaspoon Thyme
- 1 teaspoon Marjoram
- 5 Pieces pimento
- 1 Piece finely ground
- Cinnamon

Directions:

Mince pork, beef and fat through 8mm disc. Mix herbs and spices and sprinkle over meat mass and mix all together by hand for 5-10 minutes.

Fit funnel to mixer and fill pork casings. Twist into length of choice.

44. Fillet of lamb with herbs

Yield: 4 serving

Ingredient

- 450 grams Lamb neck fillet
- 1 teaspoon Dried thyme
- 1 teaspoon Dried rosemary
- 2 Cloves garlic, thinly sliced
- 2 tablespoons Olive oil
- Salt and freshly ground black pepper

Directions:

Cut each piece of lamb in half crossways then cut lengthways, not quite all the way through, and open out like a book. To cook safely on a barbecue, each piece should be no thicker than 2cm/ $\frac{3}{4}$ in. If it is any thicker, beat lightly with a rolling pin between 2 pieces of cling film

Combine all the remaining Ingredients in a bowl and add the lamb. Mix well, then cover and leave in the fridge for up to 48 hours, turning occasionally.

Place the meat on the barbecue grid and cook for 4-5 minutes each side.

Make sure it is thoroughly cooked. Brush lightly with the marinade during cooking.

HERBED VEGETABLES

45. Asparagus with herb dressing

Yield: 4 serving

Ingredient

- 1 pounds asparagus; stems peeled
- 1 if needed
- 1 juice and zest of 1 lemon
- ½ cup olive oil
- 1 tablespoon chopped fresh chives
- 1 tablespoon chopped fresh dill
- 1 tablespoon chopped fresh parsley
- 1 teaspoon chopped mint
- salt
- freshly-ground black pepper

Directions:

In a large pot of boiling salted water blanch asparagus spears until tender but not mushy. Drain and "shock" spears in ice-water to cool quickly. Drain and pat dry. In a small bowl whisk together remaining Ingredients until emulsified; season to taste with salt and pepper.

Right before serving drizzle asparagus with lemon dressing.

46. Herbed corn casserole

Yield: 1 serving

Ingredient

- 1 cup Milk
- ½ cup Mayonnaise
- 1 Egg, well beaten
- 1 can Whole kernel corn, drained
- 1 cup Herb seasoned bread stuffing mix
- 1 small Onion, minced
- 1 teaspoon Parsley flakes
- 1 cup Dry bread crumbs
- 2 tablespoons Oleo

Directions:

Combine milk and mayonnaise, mix well. Add egg, corn, stuffing, onion and parsley. Pour into greased and floured 8 inch round baking pan. Toss bread crumbs with melted oleo. Sprinkle over corn mix.

Bake at 350 degrees for 30 minutes.

47. Herbed corn scallop

Yield: 4 serving

Ingredient

- 2 Eggs
- 2 cans Cream corn (2 lb.)
- ½ cup Milk
- 4 tablespoons Melted margarine
- 2 tablespoons Minced onion
- ½ teaspoon Salt
- ¼ teaspoon Pepper
- 2 cups Ready-mix herbed seasoned stuffing

Directions:

Beat eggs slightly in a medium bowl, stir in corn, milk, butter, onion, salt and pepper. Spoon ½ of corn mixture into a greased 8 cup baking dish; sprinkle stuffing in on even layer over top; spoon remaining corn mixture over stuffing

Bake at 350 degrees for 1 hour, or until center is almost set, but still slightly moist

48. Baked herb rice with pecans

Yield: 4 serving

Ingredient

- 6 tablespoons Butter
- 1 cup Sliced fresh mushrooms
- ½ cup Chopped shallots
- 1 cup Long grain rice
- ½ cup Chopped pecans -- toasted
- 1¼ cup Broth
- Salt and freshly ground pepper
- 1 tablespoon Worcestershire sauce
- 1 teaspoon Dried thyme
- 1 teaspoon Dried rosemary
- 2 ounces Pimentos -- chopped
- 2 tablespoons Chopped -- fresh parsley
- Tabasco to taste
- 2 Bay leaves

Directions:

Preheat oven to 350 degrees. Melt butter in heavy oven-proof skillet.

Sauté mushrooms and shallots until tender

Add rice and pecans and stir until coated with butter. Add remaining Ingredients and bring to rolling boil. Remove from heat, cover and bake 1 hour or until rice is tender. Remove bay leaves; garnish with pecans and serve hot.

49. Vegetable salad

Yield: 6 serving

Ingredient

- 1½ pounds asparagus
- 3 Thin carrots, peeled
- ¼ pounds Sugar snap peas
- 1 medium Clove garlic, peeled and Minced
- 2 teaspoons Country-style Dijon mustard
- 2 tablespoons Lemon juice
- 1 tablespoon Rice or white wine vinegar
- Salt and Freshly ground pepper to Taste
- 2 tablespoons Minced herbs
- 3 Plum tomatoes, thinly sliced

Directions:

Bring a pan of water to the boil. Add the asparagus. Add the carrots and peas; time 2 minutes. Drain and plunge the vegetables into the ice water.

When the vegetables have cooled, drain and wrap in paper towels. Put into a plastic bag and refrigerate.

In a blender or small food processor combine the garlic, mustard, lemon juice and vinegar. Slowly add the oil, blending until emulsified. Add the salt, pepper and herbs.

When read to serve, combine the asparagus, carrots and peas with the tomatoes. Pour the dressing over the vegetables, stirring until well coated.

.

50. Chickpea and herb salad

Yield: 2 serving

Ingredient

- 1 can Chickpeas (16 oz.)
- 1 medium Cucumber, peeled
- 1 large Tomato
- 1 Red pepper, seeded and diced
- 2 Scallions, chopped
- 1 Avocado
- ⅓ cup Olive oil
- 1 Lemon
- ¼ teaspoon Salt
- ⅛ teaspoon White pepper
- 8 Leaves fresh basil, chopped
- ⅓ cup Dill, fresh

Directions:

Drain chickpeas and rinse well. Cut cucumber into thin slices, and then halve them. Cut tomato into wedges, and then halve them. Put cucumbers and tomato pieces, as well as red peppers and scallions, in a bowl. Set aside. Dice avocado. Put in a large bowl, and add oil and juice from half the lemon.

Add the salt, pepper and basil. Stir with fork (avocado will cream). Add the vegetables and dill to avocado mixture. Toss gently. Add chickpeas, and combine. Taste and add more lemon, salt and pepper as needed. Serve. Can be prepared ahead of time and refrigerated.

51. Summer squash soup

Yield: 1 serving

Ingredient

- 4 mediums Zucchini; wash, sliced 1"
- 1 large Yellow Crookneck Squash; wash, sliced 1"
- 1 Patty pan Squash; quartered
- 1 large Onion; thinly sliced
- 1 teaspoon Garlic; finely minced
- 3 cups Chicken Broth; defatted (3 to 3.5)
- Salt and Freshly Ground White Pepper; to taste
- 2 tablespoons Fresh Basil; finely chopped
- 2 tablespoons Fresh Parsley; finely chopped
- 1 tablespoon Lemon Juice
- 1 cup Buttermilk
- Fresh Basil; chopped
- Fresh Parsley; chopped

Directions:

In a large saucepan place all the squash. Add the onion, garlic, broth and salt and pepper; bring to a boil, cover, reduce heat and simmer for 20 to 25 minutes.

Purée in a food processor or blender with the basil, parsley and lemon juice until smooth

Stir in the buttermilk

When ready to serve, whisk until smooth and adjust the seasoning with salt and pepper.

52. Fresh herb and parmesan

Yield: 6 serving

Ingredient

- 5 cups Chicken or vegetable stock
- 3 tablespoons Olive oil
- ½ large Onion; chopped
- 1½ cup Arborio rice
- ½ cup Dry white wine
- ¾ cup Parmesan cheese; grated
- 1 cup Mixed fresh herbs
- ½ cup Roasted red peppers; chopped
- Salt and pepper; to taste

Directions:

In a small saucepan over high heat, bring the stock to a simmer. Reduce the heat to low and keep the liquid hot.

Sauté the onion, add rice and stir until a white spot appears in the center of the grains, about 1 minute. Add wine and stir until it is absorbed. Add stock slowly while stirring.

Add the $\frac{3}{4}$ cup Parmesan cheese, herbs, roasted peppers, and salt and pepper to taste. Stir to blend.

53. Herbs vegetable confetti

Yield: 1 serving

Ingredient

- 3 mediums Carrots; peeled
- 1 medium Zucchini; ends trimmed
- 1 teaspoon Olive oil
- $\frac{1}{8}$ teaspoon Ground nutmeg
- $\frac{1}{8}$ teaspoon Thyme

Directions:

Shred carrots and zucchini on the coarse side of a grater.

In a medium-size skillet, heat oil over medium-high heat. Stir in vegetables, nutmeg and thyme. Cook 3 to 4 minutes, stirring occasionally, until vegetables are wilted.

54. Bavarian herb soup

Yield: 4 serving

Ingredient

- 1 pounds Herbs
- 4 tablespoons Butter
- 1 large Onion, chopped
- 1-quart Water or vegetable stock
- 1 large Potato, peeled and chopped into small cubes
- salt and pepper
- bread cubes for croutons
- chervil, watercress, spinach, sorrel

Directions:

Melt the butter in a deep pan and fry the onion gently until transparent. Add the herbs and sweat them for a moment before you pour in the water or broth. Add the potato to the soup. Bring the soup to a boil, and then turn down the heat. Simmer for 20 minutes. Mash the potato in the soup to thicken it a little. Taste, and add salt and freshly milled pepper.

Serve with bread croutons fried in butter or bacon fat

55. Roasted herb barley

Yield: 1 serving

Ingredient

- 1 large onion
- ½ stick butter
- ½ pound fresh mushrooms, sliced
- 1 cup pearl barley
- 1 teaspoon salt
- 3 cups vegetable stock
- 1 teaspoon thyme
- ½ teaspoon marjoram
- ½ teaspoon rosemary
- ¼ teaspoon sage
- ½ teaspoon summer savory

Directions:

Chop the onion finely. In a large, oven proof pan, cook the onion in the butter for about 5 minutes until translucent. Add the mushrooms and cook for another 3 minutes. Stir in all other Ingredients except the stock, crushing the herbs before adding.

Sauté-over moderately high heat, stirring for a few minutes to coat the barley

Heat the stock in a separate pan, and add stock to barley mixture when hot.

Cover pan with foil and bake for about an hour in a preheated 350 degrees (F.) oven.

56. Cashew roast with herb stuffing

Yield: 1 Roast

Ingredient

- 2 ounces Butter
- 1 large Onion; sliced
- 8 ounces Unroasted cashew nuts
- 4 ounces White bread; crusts removed
- 2 large Garlic cloves
- Salt and Freshly ground black pepper
- Grated nutmeg
- 1 tablespoon Lemon juice
- 2 ounces Butter (or margarine)
- 1 small Onion; grated
- ½ teaspoon Thyme
- ½ teaspoon Marjoram
- 1-ounce Parsley; chopped

Directions:

Set the oven to 200C/400F/Gas Mark 6 and line a 450 g/1lb loaf tin with a long strip of non-stick paper; use some of the butter to grease the tin and paper well. Melt most of the remaining butter in a medium sized saucepan, add the onion and fry for about 10 minutes until tender but not browned. Remove from the heat.

Grind the cashew nuts in a food processor with the bread and garlic, and add to the onion, together with the water or stock, salt, pepper, grated nutmeg and lemon juice to taste. Mix all the stuffing Ingredients together.

57. Kasha with dried fruit

Yield: 6 serving

Ingredient

- 2 tablespoons Canola oil
- 1 large Onion(s), finely chopped
- 3 To 4 stalks celery
- 2 tablespoons Sage, minced
- 2 tablespoons Thyme leaves
- Salt and pepper to taste
- Peel of 1 lemon, minced
- 4 cups Cooked whole kasha groats cooked in chicken stock for extra flavor
- 1 cup Diced mixed dried fruit
- ½ cup Toasted walnuts

Directions:

Heat the oil in a large skillet and sauté, the onions, stirring occasionally, until wilted. Add the celery, sage, thyme, salt and pepper and cook, stirring, for 5 minutes more.

Stir in the lemon peel and combine with the cooked kasha. Steam the dried fruit in a vegetable steamer to soften and add along with the walnuts.

Serve hot as a side dish or use as a stuffing.

HERBED DESSERTS

58. Lemon herbal ice cream

Yield: 1 Batch

Ingredient

- 1½ cup Whipping cream
- 1½ cup Milk
- ⅔ cup Sugar
- 3 Egg yolks
- ½ teaspoon Vanilla extract
- ½ Lemon zest and Lemon juice
- ¼ cup Lemon verbena leaves
- ¼ cup Lemon balm leaves

Directions:

Stir and heat the cream, milk, and sugar until the sugar dissolves.

In a small bowl, whisk the egg yolks lightly. Pour 1 cup of the hot cream mixture into the bowl. Stir constantly with a wooden spoon. Stir in the vanilla. Stir in the lemon peel, lemon juice, and hard-packed lemon herbs into the hot ice-cream base.

Pour the mixture into an ice-cream maker and freeze according to the manufacturer's instructions.

59. Herbal jelly

Yield: 8 Half-pints

Ingredient

- 1½ cup Herb leaves, fresh
- 3½ cup Sugar
- 1 drop Food colouring, green
- 2¼ cup; Water, cold
- 2 tablespoons Lemon juice
- Pectin, liquid; pouch + 2 t.

Directions:

Combine herb and water in a saucepan; bring to a full boil, covered, and remove from the heat to let steep 15 minutes. Ladle into a jelly bag and let drip for one hour. You should have 1-¾ cups of infusion.

Combine the infusion, lemon juice, sugar, and food colouring and cook over high heat until at a full rolling boil. Add liquid pectin, and bring to a full rolling boil again, stirring constantly.

Remove from the heat, skim froth, and ladle into sterilized half-pint jelly jars, leaving $\frac{1}{4}$" Head space. Process as for fruit jellies

60. Herbal lemon cookies

Yield: 1 batch

Ingredient

- 1 cup Butter
- 2 cups Sugar; divided
- 2 Eggs
- 1 teaspoon Vanilla extract
- 2½ cup Flour
- 2 teaspoons Baking powder
- ¼ teaspoon Salt
- ⅓ cup Dried lemon herbs
- ⅓ cup total: Herbs

Directions:

Cream butter and 1¾ cups sugar

Add eggs and vanilla; beat well.

Combine the flour, baking powder, salt and herbs. Add to creamed mixture; mix.

Drop dough by teaspoonfuls, 3" apart, on a greased cookie sheet.

Bake at 350 F. for 8 to 10 minutes, or until barely browned. Cool slightly, then remove to a rack.

61. Chicken pot pie with herbs

Yield: 4 serving

Ingredient

- 2 tablespoons Butter
- 1 Onion, chopped
- ½ teaspoon Minced fresh sage and thyme
- 2 teaspoons Minced fresh garlic
- 2 tablespoons Minced green pepper
- 2 tablespoons Flour
- 1½ to 1 3/4 cups chicken stock
- 2 cups Cooked chicken
- 1 tablespoon Chopped sweet marjoram
- 1 cup Yellow turnip
- 2 cups Waxy potatoes
- 2 cups Carrots, peeled and cut
- Salt, Cayenne pepper

Directions:

Melt the butter in a heavy saucepan and add the onion, sage and thyme. Stir in the garlic and green pepper.

Cook the turnip and potatoes in boiling water for 5 minutes. Add the carrots and cook for 3 minutes more.

Cut in the shortening. Stir in the milk with a fork. Pat the dough together. Pat the dough to a 1-inch thickness. Cut the biscuits with a biscuit cutter.

62. Herbed popover mix

Yield: 1 serving

Ingredient

- 2 cups Flour
- 1 teaspoon Salt
- ¼ teaspoon Thyme
- ¼ teaspoon Crumbled sage POPOVERS:
- 8 tablespoons Butter
- 1 pack Mix
- 2 cups Milk
- 6 Eggs
- Mix: Combine and store in an airtight container.

Directions:

Herbed Popovers: Preheat oven to 400 and place butter in each of 8 custard cups or popover molds. Place in oven to melt the butter.

In a large bowl, combine mix, milk and eggs and stir with a wire whisk until smooth. Pour into the prepared cups until ⅔ full.

HERBED BREADS

63. Herb rolls

Yield: 12 serving

Ingredient

- 4 tablespoons Butter or margarine
- 3 tablespoons Finely chopped onion
- 1 Clove garlic; minced
- ¾ teaspoon Dried oregano
- ¾ teaspoon Dried basil
- ¾ teaspoon Dried tarragon
- 1 cup Water
- 3 cups All-purpose flour
- 1 teaspoon Salt
- 1½ teaspoon Sugar
- 1½ teaspoon Red Star yeast

Directions:

Melt the butter. Add the onion, garlic, and herbs. Sauté over medium heat

Place all Ingredients in the bread pan and select Dough setting, press Start.

Turn out dough and gently roll and stretch dough into a 24-inch rope.

With a sharp knife, divide dough into 18 pieces. Roll into balls and place in a greased muffin tins. Bake in 400~ oven 12- 15 min until golden

64. Garden herb bread

Yield: 8 serving

Ingredient

- ¾ cup Water
- 2 cups White bread flour
- 1 tablespoon Dry milk
- 1 tablespoon Sugar
- 1 teaspoon Salt
- 1 tablespoon Butter
- 3 cups White bread flour
- 2 tablespoons Dry milk
- 2 tablespoons Sugar
- 1½ teaspoon Salt
- 2 tablespoons Butter
- 1 teaspoon Chives/Marjoram/Thyme
- ½ teaspoon Basil
- 2 teaspoons Active-dry yeast

Directions:

The fragrance of turkey stuffing will fill your home while this flavourful bread is baking, thanks to all those aromatic dried herbs.

This loaf is excellent for any cold meat sandwich you can dream up including turkey and cranberry. It also makes tasty croutons.

Follow the directions for your bread machine.

65. Lavender herb bread

Yield: 1 loaf

Ingredient

- 1 pack Active dry yeast
- ¼ cup; Warm water
- 1 cup Low-fat cottage cheese
- ¼ cup Honey
- 2 tablespoons Butter
- 1 teaspoon Dried lavender buds
- 1 tablespoon Fresh lemon thyme
- ½ tablespoon Fresh basil; finely chopped
- ¼ teaspoon Baking soda
- 2 Eggs
- 2½ cup Unbleached flour
- Butter

Directions:

In a small bowl, dissolve yeast in water.

In a larger bowl, mix together the cottage cheese, honey, butter, herbs, baking soda and eggs. Stir in the yeast mixture. Gradually add flour to form stiff dough, beating well after each addition.

Cover and let rise about 1 hour, or until doubled in bulk.

Stir the dough down with a spoon. Place in a well-greased casserole

Bake at 350 F. for one hour for a large loaf, 20 to 30 minutes for small loaves

66. Cheddar wheat herb crescents

Ingredient

- 2¾ cup Milk
- 1 tablespoon Sugar
- 1 pack Active dry yeast
- 5½ cup Whole wheat flour
- 2 teaspoons Salt
- 1 Eggs
- 3 tablespoons Butter
- ¾ cup Flour
- 1½ cup Grated cheddar cheese
- 2 tablespoons Sesame seeds
- 1 tablespoon Dried basil and 1 tablespoon oregano
- Lemon juice

Directions:

Stir the milk and sugar in a large bowl, sprinkle on yeast, let soften. Beat in $3\frac{1}{2}$ cups flour, cover, let rest 15 minutes. Beat in the salt and egg, and then add the butter. Turn out and knead on floured board 10 minutes. Place in greased bowl, turn, cover, let rise until double.

Punch down dough, gradually kneading in the cheese. Divide dough into fourths. Roll each into a circle

Spread rolled dough with herb butter, cut into wedges, roll up, put on baking sheet. Cover loosely. Repeat with remaining dough. Bake at 375 degrees F, 25 minutes.

67. Corn meal herb bread

Yield: 1 serving

Ingredient

- 1 pack (5/16-oz.) yeast
- 1 cup Unbleached flour
- ¾ cup Bread flour
- ½ cup White or yellow cornmeal
- 4 tablespoons Fresh, chopped herbs
- 1 tablespoon Vegetable oil
- 1 teaspoon Salt
- 1 tablespoon Sugar
- ⅞ cup Water
- Chives, cilantro, Italian parsley, or basil, OR 4 teaspoons dry herbs.

Directions:

Put all Ingredients, in the order given, into the bread machine, select WHITE bread, and push Start.

Serve warm with sweet butter.

68. Country herb crescents

Yield: 8 serving

Ingredient

- 1 can(8oz.) Pillsbury Crescent
- Dinner Rolls
- 1 tablespoon Dairy sour cream
- ½ teaspoon Instant minced or chopped
- Onion
- ½ teaspoon dried parsley flakes
- ½ teaspoon Ground sage
- ¼ teaspoon Celery salt

Directions:

Unroll dough; separate into 8 triangles. Combine remaining Ingredients; spread evenly over each triangle. Roll, place and bake Crescents as directed on package label.

HERBED CONDIMENTS

69. Herbal seasoning

Yield: 1 serving

Ingredient

- ½ teaspoon Ground hot pepper
- 1 tablespoon Garlic powder
- 1 teaspoon Each dried basil, dried Marjoram, dried thyme, dried Parsley,
- Dried savory, mace, onion Powder, freshly ground black Pepper, Powdered sage.

Directions:

Combine Ingredients, Store in airtight container in cool dry, dark place up to six months.

70. Ethiopian herb mix (berbere)

Yield: 1 serving

Ingredient

- 2 teaspoons Whole cumin seeds
- 4 each Whole cloves
- ¾ teaspoon Black cardamom seeds
- ½ teaspoon Whole black peppercorns
- ¼ teaspoon Whole allspice
- 1 teaspoon Fenugreek seeds
- ½ teaspoon Whole coriander seeds
- 10 smalls Dried red chilies
- ½ teaspoon Grated ginger
- ¼ teaspoon Turmeric
- 2½ tablespoon Sweet Hungarian paprika
- ⅛ teaspoon Cinnamon
- ⅛ teaspoon Ground cloves

Directions:

In a small frying pan, on a low heat, toast cumin, cloves, cardamom, peppercorns, allspice, fenugreek and coriander for about 2 minutes, stirring constantly

Remove from heat and cool for 5 minutes. Discard stems from chilies. In a spice grinder or with a mortar and pestle, finely grind together the toasted spices and chilies.

Mix in remaining Ingredients.

71. Herb salad dressing mix

Yield: 1 serving

Ingredient

- ¼ cup Parsley flakes
- 2 tablespoons Each dried oregano, basil and marjoram, crumbled
- 2 tablespoons Sugar
- 1 tablespoon Fennel seeds, crushed
- 1 tablespoon Dry mustard
- 1½ teaspoon Black pepper

Directions:

Place all the Ingredients in a 1-pint jar, cover tightly and shake well to mix. Store in a cool, dark, dry place

Makes 1 cup to Make Herbal Vinaigrette Dressing: In a small bowl, whisk together 1 tablespoons Herb Salad dressing mix, ¾ cup warm water, 2½ tablespoons tarragon vinegar or white wine vinegar, 1 tablespoon olive oil and 1 crushed clove garlic.

Taste and add $\frac{1}{4}$ to $\frac{1}{2}$ teaspoon of the Herb Salad Dressing Mix if you want a stronger flavor. Let Stand at room temperature at least 30 minutes before using, then whisk again.

72. Mixed herb vinegar

Yield: 1 serving

Ingredient

- 1-pint Red wine vinegar
- 1 Piece cider vinegar
- 2 Peeled, halved garlic cloves
- 1 Branch tarragon
- 1 Sprig thyme
- 2 Sprigs fresh oregano
- 1 small Stalk sweet basil
- 6 Black peppercorns

Directions:

Pour red wine and cider vinegar into a quart jar. Add garlic, herbs, peppercorns and cover. Let stand in a cool place, out of the sun, for three weeks. Shake occasionally. Pour into bottles and stop with cork.

73. Mixed herb pesto

Yield: 1 serving

Ingredient

- 1 cup Packed fresh flat-leafed parsley
- ½ cup Packed fresh basil leaves;
- 1 tablespoon Fresh thyme leaves
- 1 tablespoon Fresh rosemary leaves
- 1 tablespoon Fresh tarragon leaves
- ½ cup Freshly grated parmesan
- ⅓ cup Olive oil
- ¼ cup Walnuts; toasted golden
- 1 tablespoon Balsamic vinegar

Directions:

In a food processor blend together all Ingredients with salt and pepper to taste until smooth. (Pesto keeps, surface covered with plastic wrap, chilled, 1 week.)

74. Mustard-herb marinade

Yield: 1 serving

Ingredient

- ½ cup Dijon Mustard
- 2 tablespoons Dry mustard
- 2 tablespoons Vegetable oil
- ¼ cup Dry white wine
- 2 tablespoons Dried tarragon
- 2 tablespoons Dried thyme
- 2 tablespoons Dried sage, crushed

Directions:

Mix all of the Ingredients in a bowl. Let stand 1 hour. Add chicken or fish and coat well. Let stand in marinade. Pat dry with paper towels

Use the remaining marinade to baste fish or chicken just before removing from the grill.

75. Herbal dessert sauce

Yield: 1 serving

Ingredient

- ⅓ cup Heavy cream
- ¾ cup Buttermilk
- 1 teaspoon Grated lemon rind
- ¼ teaspoon Ground ginger
- ⅛ teaspoon Ground cardamom
- ¼ cup Garam masala, allspice or
- Nutmeg

Directions:

Whip the cream in a medium-sized, chilled bowl until soft peaks form.

Mix remaining Ingredients together in a small bowl and gently fold into the cream. The sauce should be the consistency of thick cream.

76. Citrus herb dressing

Yield: 1 serving

Ingredient

- ½ medium Sized red bell pepper,
- 2 mediums Tomatoes, cut up
- ½ cup Loosely packed fresh basil
- 2 Cloves garlic, minced
- ½ cup Fresh orange juice
- ½ cup Loosely packed fresh Parsley
- ¼ cup Raspberry vinegar
- 1 tablespoon Dry mustard
- 2 teaspoons Fresh thyme leaves
- 2 teaspoons Fresh tarragon
- 2 teaspoons Fresh oregano
- Ground black pepper

Directions:

Combine all Ingredients in a blender or food processor and blend until puréed.

77. Cottage-herb dressing

Yield: 6 servings

Ingredient

- 1 tablespoon Milk
- 12 ounces Cottage Cheese
- 1 teaspoon Lemon Juice
- 1 small Onion Slice -- Thin
- 3 Radishes -- Halved
- 1 teaspoon Mixed Salad Herbs
- 1 Parsley Sprig
- ¼ teaspoon Salt

Directions:

Put the milk, cottage cheese and lemon juice in a blender container and blend until smooth. Add the remaining Ingredients to the cottage cheese mixture and blend until all of the vegetables are chopped.

78. Herbes de provence mix

Yield: 1 serving

Ingredient

- ½ cup Dried whole thyme
- ¼ cup Whole dried basil
- 2 tablespoons Whole dried oregano
- 2 tablespoons Whole dried rosemary

Mix Spices, together thoroughly. Store in an airtight container

79. Herb and oil marinade

Yield: 1 serving

Ingredient

- Juice and rind of 1 orange
- ¼ cup Lemon juice
- ¼ cup Vegetable oil
- ½ teaspoon Ginger
- ½ teaspoon Sage
- 1 Clove of garlic, minced
- Freshly ground pepper

Directions:

Combine Ingredients. Allow meat to marinate in shallow glass dish for 4 hours in refrigerator. Baste with marinade during broiling or barbecuing.

80. Easy herb vinegars

Yield: 1 serving

Ingredient

- 4 sprigs fresh rosemary

Directions:

To make herb vinegar, put rinsed and dried herbs and any spices into a sterilized 750-ml wine bottle and add about 3 cups vinegar, filling to within $\frac{1}{4}$ inch of the top. Stop with a new cork and set aside for 2 to 3 weeks to steep. The vinegar has a shelf life of at least 1 year.

With red wine vinegar, use: 4 sprigs fresh curly-leaf parsley, 2 Tablespoons black peppercorns

81. Sorrel-chive pesto

Yield: 1 serving

Ingredient

- 1 cup Sorrel
- 4 tablespoons Shallots; finely minced
- 4 tablespoons Pine nuts; ground
- 3 tablespoons Parsley; chopped
- 3 tablespoons Chives; chopped
- Grated peel of 4 oranges
- ¼ Onions, red; chopped
- 1 tablespoon Mustard, dry
- 1 teaspoon Salt
- 1 teaspoon Pepper, black
- 1 pinch Pepper, cayenne
- ¾ cup Oil, olive

Directions:

Blend the sorrel, shallots, pine nuts, parsley, chives, orange peel and onion in a food processor or blender.

Add dry mustard, salt, pepper and cayenne, and mix again. SLOWLY drizzle in the oil while the blade is moving.

Transfer to tempered glass jars.

82. Cucumber herb dressing

Yield: 12 servings

Ingredient

- ½ cup Parsley
- 1 tablespoon Fresh dill, minced
- 1 teaspoon Fresh tarragon, minced
- 2 tablespoons Apple juice concentrate
- 1 medium Cucumber, peeled, seeded
- 1 clove Garlic, minced
- 2 Green onions
- 1½ teaspoon White wine vinegar
- ½ cup Low-fat yogurt
- ¼ teaspoon Dijon mustard

Directions:

Combine all Ingredients except yogurt and mustard in blender. Blend until smooth, stir in yogurt and mustard. Store in refrigerator

83. Herbed pecan rub

Yield: 1 serving

Ingredient

- ½ cup Pecans -- broken
- 3 Cloves garlic -- cut up
- ½ cup Fresh oregano
- ½ cup Fresh thyme
- ½ teaspoon Lemon peel
- ½ teaspoon Black pepper
- ¼ teaspoon Salt
- ¼ cup Cooking oil

Directions:

In a blender or food processor, combine all Ingredients EXCEPT oil.

Cover and blend several times, scraping sides, until a paste forms.

With machine running, gradually add oil until mixture forms a paste.

Rub onto fish or chicken.

84. Zesty herb dressing

Yield: 1

Ingredient

- ¾ cup white grape juice; or apple juice
- ¼ cup white wine vinegar
- 2 tablespoons powdered fruit pectin
- 1 teaspoon Dijon mustard
- 2 cloves garlic; crushed
- 1 teaspoon dried onion flakes
- ½ teaspoon dried basil
- ½ teaspoon dried oregano
- ¼ teaspoon black pepper; coarsely ground

Directions:

In small bowl, combine grape juice, vinegar and pectin; stir until pectin is dissolved. Stir in mustard and remaining Ingredients; mix well. Store in refrigerator

85. Garlic-lemon-herb rub

Yield: 1 serving

Ingredient

- ¼ cup Garlic; minced
- ¼ cup Lemon zest; grated
- ½ cup Parsley; fresh, chopped fine
- 2 tablespoons Thyme; fresh chopped
- 2 tablespoons Rosemary
- 2 tablespoons Sage; fresh, chopped
- ½ cup Olive oil

Directions:

In a small bowl, combine Ingredients and mix well. Use the day it is mixed.

86. Dolce latté herb dip

Yield: 6 servings

Ingredient

- 450 milliliters Soured cream
- 150 grams dolce latté; crumbled
- 1 tablespoon Lemon juice
- 4 tablespoons Mayonnaise
- 2 tablespoons Mild curry paste
- 1 Red pepper; diced
- 1 50 grams full fat soft cheese; (2oz.)
- 1 small Onion; finely diced
- 2 tablespoons mixed herbs
- 2 tablespoons Tomato purée
- Salt and freshly ground black pepper
- Vegetable crudités and sliced pita bread

Directions:

Divide the soured cream between 3 small bowls. To one bowl, add the dolce latté and lemon juice, to the second bowl, add 2 tablespoons mayonnaise, curry paste and red pepper. To the third bowl add the full fat soft cheese, onion, herbs and tomato purée.

Add seasoning to taste to each of the bowls and mix well. Transfer the dips to serving dishes and serve chilled with vegetable crudités and sliced pita bread.

87.French herb blend

Yield: 2 cups

Ingredient

- ½ cup Tarragon
- ½ cup Chervil
- 2 tablespoons Sage leaves
- ½ cup Thyme
- 2 tablespoons Rosemary
- 5 tablespoons Chives
- 2 tablespoons Orange rind, desiccated
- 2 tablespoons Celery seed, ground

Directions:

Dump everything together and mix until well-combined. Pack into small jars and label

Crumble spices in hand when using.

Measure spices by volume, not by weight, because of the large variation in moisture content.

88. Herb and spice butter

Yield: 1 serving

Ingredient

- 8 tablespoons butter softened
- 2 tablespoons Fresh rosemary, chopped
- 1 tablespoon Fresh tarragon, chopped
- 1 tablespoon Fresh chives, chopped
- 1 tablespoon Curry powder

Directions:

Beat the softened butter until creamy. Blend in remaining Ingredients.

Place the butter on waxed paper and form it into a roll with a flat-bladed knife.

Allow the butter to rest in the refrigerator for at least two hours so the butter will completely absorb the flavor of the herbs.

89. Herbal vegetable dressing

Yield: 1 serving

Ingredient

- ½ teaspoon Fresh parsley
- ½ teaspoon Fresh tarragon
- ½ teaspoon Fresh chives
- ½ teaspoon Fresh chervil
- 3 tablespoons Wine vinegar
- 9 tablespoons Olive oil
- 1 teaspoon Dijon mustard
- ½ teaspoon Salt
- ½ teaspoon Black pepper

Directions:

Mince the fresh herbs, reserving a few leaves to use as garnishes.

Place all Ingredients in a small mixing bowl.. Beat vigorously with a wire whisk until well blended.

Garnish with fresh leaves and serve immediately.

90. Bacon, tomato and herb dip

Yield: 1 serving

Ingredient

- 1 Container; (16 oz.) sour cream
- 1 tablespoon Basil
- 1 tablespoon Beau Monde Seasoning
- 1 medium Tomato
- 8 slices Bacon-cooked and crumbled

Directions:

In medium bowl, stir together all Ingredients until well blended. Cover and chill 2 hours or overnight.

91. Garlic herb spread

Yield: 8 serving

Ingredient

- 1 Head garlic
- 4 Sun-dried tomatoes; not packed in oil
- 1 cup Nonfat yogurt cheese
- $\frac{1}{2}$ teaspoon Maple syrup
- 2 tablespoons Fresh basil; chopped
- $\frac{1}{2}$ teaspoon Red pepper flakes
- $\frac{1}{4}$ teaspoon Sea salt; freshly ground
- Loaf of Italian bread; sliced; optional

Directions:

Wrap the garlic head in aluminum foil and bake in a preheated 375F oven for 35 minutes.

Bring the sun-dried tomatoes to a boil in a small amount of water. Let sit for 15 minutes, and then drain on paper towels. Chop finely when dried.

Combine all the Ingredients except the bread with a wire whisk. Allow to sit for at least 30 minutes.

92. Chevre with herbs spread

Yield: 8 serving

Ingredient

- 4 ounces Plain cream cheese
- 4 ounces Chevre
- Fresh Herbs -- to taste

Directions:

If you are using your own herbs, rosemary, tarragon, and summer savory are good choices, alone or in combination.

Use the spread to stuff snow or sugar snap peas, spread on cucumber or zucchini rounds, sweet meal biscuits, water biscuits, or slightly toasted miniature bagels.

HERBED DRINKS

93. Spicy herbal liqueur

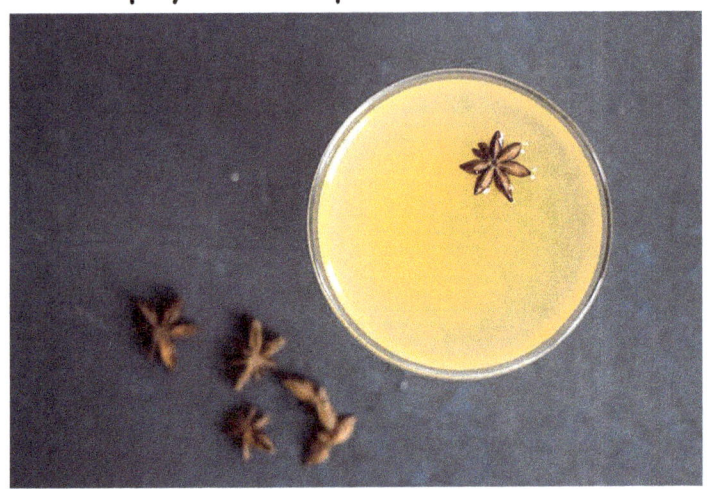

Yield: 1 Quart

Ingredient

- 6 Cardamom pods
- 3 teaspoons Anise seeds
- $2\frac{1}{4}$ teaspoon Chopped angelica root
- 1 Cinnamon stick
- 1 Clove
- $\frac{1}{4}$ teaspoon Mace
- 1 Fifth of vodka
- 1 cup Sugar syrup
- Container: 1/2-gallon jar

Directions:

Remove seeds from cardamom pods. Add the anise seeds, and crush all the kernels with the back of a fork.

Put them in a 1-quart container adding angelica root, cinnamon stick, clove, mace, and vodka.

Shake mixture well and store in a cupboard for 1 week. Pour through cheesecloth lined strainer several times. Blend the liquid with the sugar syrup. Ready to serve

94. Fruited herbal iced tea

Yield: 1 serving

Ingredient

- 1 Bag Tazo Passion tea
- 1-quart Water
- 2 cups Fresh orange juice
- Orange wheel
- Mint leaves

Directions:

Place tea bag in 1 quart of boiling water and let steep for 5 minutes.

Remove tea bag. Pour tea into a 1-gallon pitcher filled with ice. Once the ice melts, fill the remaining space in the pitcher with water.

Fill a cocktail shaker with one half of brewed tea and one half orange juices. Shake well and strain into an ice filled tumbler glass. Garnish with orange wheel and mint leaves.

95.Ice herbal cooler

Yield: 6 servings

Ingredient

- 4 cups Boiling water;
- 8 Red Zinger tea bags
- 12 ounces apple juice concentrate
- Juice of 1 orange
- 1 Lemon; sliced
- 1 Orange; sliced

Directions:

Pour the boiling water over the tea bags. Let the tea steep until the water is lukewarm, making a very strong tea. In a large pitcher, combine tea, apple juice and orange juice. Garnish the pitcher with lemon and oranges slices. Pour into glasses filled with ice, and garnish with mint.

Yield: 1 serving

Ingredient

- Bag of dried lime flowers
- Boiling water

Directions:

Simply put dried flowers, one small handful to the average teapot, in the pot. Pour in the boiling water and stir well. Serve.

Do not allow steeping for longer than four minutes as the flavor will be lost.

96. Raspberry herbal tea

Yield: 8 servings

Ingredient

- 2 Family-size raspberry tea bags
- 2 Blackberry tea teabags
- 2 Black currant tea teabags
- 1 Bottle sparkling apple cider
- ½ cup Juice concentrate
- ½ cup Orange juice
- ½ cup Sugar

Directions:

Place all the Ingredients in a large pitcher. Chill. We serve ours with fruited ice cubes.

Reserve enough juices to fill an ice-cube tray and we place slices of strawberries and blueberries into each cube.

97. Cardamom tea

Yield: 1 serving

Ingredient

- 15 Cardamom Seeds water
- ½ cup Milk
- 2 drops Vanilla (to 3 drops)
- Honey

Directions:

For indigestion, mix 15 pulverized seeds in ½ cup hot water. Add 1 ounce of fresh ginger root and a cinnamon stick.

Simmer 15 minutes over low heat. Add ½ cup milk and simmer 10 more minutes. Add 2 to 3 drops of vanilla. Sweeten with honey. Drink 1 to 2 cups daily.

98. Sassafras Tea

SERVES: 10

Ingredients

- 4 sassafras roots
- 2quarts water
- sugar or honey

Directions:

Wash roots and cut saplings off where they're green and where the root ends.

Bring water to a boil and add roots.

Simmer until the water is a deep brownish red (the darker the stronger -- I like mine strong).

Strain into a pitcher through wire and a coffee filter if you don't want any sediment.

Add honey or sugar to taste.

Serve hot or cold with lemon and a sprig of mint.

99. Moringa Tea

Servings: 2

Ingredients

- 800 ml Water
- 5-6 Mint leaves - torn
- 1 teaspoon Cumin Seeds
- 2 teaspoon Moringa Powder
- 1 tablespoon Lime / Lemon Juice
- 1 teaspoon Organic Honey as sweetener

Directions:

Bring 4 cups of water to rolling boil.

Add 5-6 mint leaves and 1 teaspoon of cumin seeds / jeera.

Let it boil until water is reduced to half the quantity.

When water reduces to half, add 2 teaspoons of Moringa powder.

Regulate the heat to high, when it froths and comes up, turn off the heat.

Cover with a lid and let it sit for 4-5 minutes.

After 5 minutes, strain tea into a cup.

Add organic honey to taste and squeeze in fresh lime juice.

100. Sage Tea

Ingredients

- 6 fresh sage leaves, left on stem
- Boiling water
- Honey (or agave syrup for vegan)
- 1 lemon wedge

Directions

Bring the water to a boil.

Wash the sage thoroughly.

Place the sage in a mug, and pour over the boiling water. Allow the herbs to steep for 5 minutes. (Alternate method: If you prefer, you can also chop the sage leaves and place them in a tea strainer before steeping.)

Remove the sage. Stir in a drizzle of honey and a squeeze of lemon (required for the best flavor).

CONCLUSION

To clean fresh herbs, dunk them in a cold water bath and gently move them around in the water to remove any dirt or debris. Shake off the excess water, and carefully pat the herbs dry with paper towels. More delicate herbs like parsley, cilantro, and chervil should be handled gently, in comparison to sturdy herbs like sprigs of rosemary and thyme.

To store use a plastic bag or in a jar filled with water. Leafy herbs can be stored upright in a jar of water, with the leaves sticking out of the top of the jar. All herbs can also be stored between a damp paper towels in an airtight plastic bag in the refrigerator.

ENJOY COOKING WITH HERBS!

www.ingramcontent.com/pod-product-compliance
Lightning Source LLC
Chambersburg PA
CBHW070646120526
44590CB00013BA/847